# TINI BIGS BIG MARTINIS

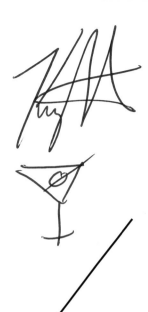

By Keith Robbins and
Patrick Haight
Foreword

BY

G

•

M

•

FORD

**PHOTOGRAPHY BY ANGIE NORWOOD BROWNE AND JAIMIE TRUEBLOOD**

DOCUMENTARY MEDIA LLC SEATTLE, WASHINGTON

Tini Bigs Big Martinis
Copyright © 2005
Documentary Media
and Tini Bigs Lounge

First edition 2005
Printed in China

by Keith Robbins
and Patrick Haight
Foreword by G. M. Ford

Library of Congress Cataloguing-in-Publication Data

Robbins, Keith, 1958-
Tini Bigs big martinis / by Keith Robbins;
foreword by G. M. Ford. — 1st ed.
p. cm.

ISBN 0-9719084-8-6
1. Martinis. I. Title.
TX951.R62 2005
641.8'74—dc22

2005009911

Recipes: Tini Bigs staff
Recipe Testing: Keith Robbins
Patrick Haight
Matt Dickinson
Managing Editor: Petyr Beck
Drink Photographer: Angie Norwood Browne
Drink Stylist: Patty Wittmann
Photography: Jaimie Trueblood
Angie Norwood Browne
Editors: Judy Gouldthorpe
Hillary Self
Designer: Nancy Gellos
Project Manager: Jody Ericson Dorow

Documentary Media LLC
3250 41st Avenue SW
Seattle, Washington 98116
(206) 935-9292
email: books@docbooks.com
www.documentarymedia.com

## TABLE OF CONTENTS

# FOREWORD

*"Love may be blind, but marriage is a real eye-opener."*
~ G. M. Ford

I met my wife at Tini Bigs. Of course, I'd seen her before at the U Dub, where we both taught writing classes. Cute little bird of a woman, looked like she'd break in half if you stood too close to her. Not only that but she was always talking to somebody, which was exactly what I was always trying to avoid, so, although we'd spent a fair amount of time in the same room, we'd never actually made contact.

I'd been teaching the mystery-writing classes for about five years when I decided I'd had enough and needed somebody to palm my classes off on. Since Skye was a well-known writer and was already teaching one of the sections, she seemed like a target-rich environment. The plan was to ply her with a few drinks, slip her the program and be on my way. When she said she wanted to meet somewhere in her neighborhood, I said fine. She suggested Tini Bigs. No problem. Seven o'clock. See you there.

I remember the night like it was yesterday. It was raining buckets, so I cabbed it down from Capitol Hill to find her already ensconced at a table, waiting for me. She was even smaller than I remembered, so I figured this wasn't going to take long. Coupla sissy drinks . . . pour her into a cab and make it back to my place in time for the second half of Monday Night Football. Life was good.

I'm a martini drinker. Bombay Sapphire . . . three olives, and, I can pour 'em down with the best of them, a circumstance which merely serves to underline the fact that a man of my vast experience should have seen it coming. The minute she ordered that first double Dalwhinnie on the rocks, I shoulda sensed that life as I knew it was over.

Four hours and a hefty-sized tab later, we were still chatting away as we ambled across the street to the local greasy spoon. The rest, as they say, is history.

# INTRODUCTION

I'm often asked, "Who is Mr. Bigs?" A look into the mirrors of the classic back bar at Tini Bigs will give you a hint. I fell in love with the back bar when I first saw it in the old Watertown Tavern, in the Belltown area of downtown Seattle. Built in 1909 by the Brunswick-Balke-Collender Company, this was a piece of history that was meant to be the centerpiece of a great classic bar.

That back bar had stood at the corner of First and Bell since before Prohibition, and I could imagine the characters who must have been served spirits there. Certainly some were well-to-do businessmen looking for a medicinal tonic. In the 1920s, perhaps the back bar was accessible only to shadowy men and disreputable women who looked over their shoulders as they gave the secret knock. And later, locals may have met to shake their heads over recent news events, to welcome back soldiers and to comfort widows, to celebrate progress and to commiserate over losses. All these experiences had been absorbed by its wood and recorded by its mirrors. This was too great a focal point to leave behind, so when the Watertown's building was closed to be converted into low-income housing, I crated up the back bar to save it until I could find the perfect location.

The Brunswick-Balke-Collender Company began in Cincinnati with John Moses Brunswick, an immigrant from Switzerland who established the Cincinnati Carriage Making Company in 1845. As the company's reputation grew, Brunswick found a niche crafting exceptional billiard tables and, after a merger with rivals, high-quality front and back bars. The bars' ornate detail and fine woodwork quickly made them popular throughout the world and in the finest lounges.

I'd had my eye on the corner of First and Denny for a while when, in December 1990, I had the opportunity to acquire the First Avenue side, where I started a bar called the Romper Room. At that time, the corner space next door was occupied by a travel agency, but I had visions of a perfect bar location as I negotiated the right of first refusal. When the space became available in 1996, I knew that it was time to resurrect the back bar after its seven years in storage. It had been gone but not forgotten; it whispered to me over those seven years, longing for a return to its former glory. I installed it in its new home and built a classic corner lounge around it, using the mystique of the martini as my inspiration.

Initially, I thought we would prepare numerous classic martini-age cocktails, and with the help of the most amazing opening staff of bartenders (Chris, Joe, Jude and Barry), the list of martinis grew. When the list exceeded twenty, I knew the focus for the bar had to be The Martini — or at least cocktails that were served in triangle-shaped glasses. (We all know there is only one Martini.) At Tini Bigs we have our own idea about what a martini is and what it should taste like. Hell, we have strong ideas about everything! That's not to be confused with what a classic martini is or what the original martini was. We'll put ours up against anyone's. But the best martini is the one made exactly the way you like it to be made. And we'll do that for you. That's our business — the best bartenders making your perfect martini from the finest spirits available. Still, no matter what you call your favorite, the draw of the martini is undeniable. To some, it was even powerful enough to risk prison for.

During Prohibition, the bootleggers determined what people were drinking. Whiskey fell from favor because of its long and complicated aging process. Gin, on the other hand, could be easily made by combining the ingredients in any available container — even a bathtub. So the martini naturally rose in popularity, and its praises were sung by many writers and noted personalities. When Prohibition came to an end in 1933, the martini remained popular with the new crowd frequenting the now-legal drinking establishments. It was still not considered proper for women to accept drinks from the bar, though, and so the cocktail lounge emerged with the addition of tables and waiter service. The once seedy had now become classy, but the ambience still hinted at the recent perilous past.

These qualities were what I found so enchanting about the martini and the back bar. The classic corner lounge had to embody all of these elements. The back bar immediately dictated the décor. I added tables and chairs and intimate booths, niches perfect for sipping martinis and carefully eyeing one's fellow patrons. A kind of catwalk divides the lounge, allowing the still popular art of seeing and being seen to flourish. Next came a Victorian-style tin ceiling, a decorative element that was very popular in America in the 1870s through the 1890s, just as the martini was invented and enjoying early fame. And to pay homage to the illicit era of the martini's history, red lights near the ceiling reflect off the tin and cast a sensuous glow over the bar and its patrons.

**W**ith the classic lounge in place and the menu of cocktails solidified, I decided to serve unabashedly large martinis. There is nothing shy and understated about the martini; it is a drink that refuses to be self-conscious — so that was what I was going to call the establishment: Big Tinis. But I soon realized that the name was too obvious and not reflective of the classic, checkered past of the martini that the back bar embodied. "What about Tini Bigs?" I asked my friend Adam, who likes his cocktails. The response was immediate: "A little retro, a little dark, and seedy."

**S**o who is Mr. Bigs? Maybe he sat in front of that back bar, savoring the liquor that had never tasted so sweet when it was legal. Maybe he was the last loyal regular before I resurrected the back bar, watching his reflection as he lowered the final empty glass. Or maybe Mr. Bigs is every man and woman who still approaches the back bar to receive the best-quality spirits in an atmosphere befitting the historic, and sometimes dark, legacy of liquor.

Keith Robbins

## Original Martini (Martinez, California, circa late 1800s)

3 1/2 ounces Plymouth gin
1 1/2 ounces French (dry) vermouth
2 to 3 drops of bitters

Fill a cocktail shaker with ice. Pour in gin,
vermouth and bitters. Stir and strain into
a big martini glass.*

## Tini Bigs Classic Dry Martini

4 ounces Bombay Sapphire gin or Finlandia vodka
Spritz of dry vermouth

Garnish: 3 olives

Fill a cocktail shaker with ice. Add gin or vodka.
Shake vigorously or stir, depending on your
preference. Place vermouth in an atomizer* and
lightly spray the inside of an empty big martini
glass. Strain the contents of the cocktail shaker into
the glass. Garnish with olives.

*See glossary.

## Chi-Town Tini

4 ounces Finlandia vodka or Tanqueray gin

Garnish: 3 blue-cheese-stuffed olives

Fill a cocktail shaker with ice. Add vodka or gin. Shake vigorously and strain into a big martini glass.* Garnish with olives.

*See glossary.

## Gibson

Garnish: 3 cocktail onions

## Dirty-Tini

Add olive juice to taste.

Garnish: 3 green olives

Thanks to those from the Windy City.

## Tini Bigs Manhattan

3 ounces Woodford Reserve bourbon
$\frac{1}{2}$ ounce sweet vermouth
2 drops of Angostura bitters

Garnish: maraschino cherry

Fill a cocktail shaker with ice.
Add bourbon, vermouth and bitters.
Shake vigorously and strain into
a big martini glass.* Garnish with
a maraschino cherry.

*See glossary.

# Blue Sky Martini

4 ounces Finlandia vodka
Splash ($1/4$ ounce) of Grand Marnier
$1/2$ ounce blue Curaçao

Garnish: lemon twist*

Fill a cocktail shaker with ice. Add vodka
and Grand Marnier. Stir and let stand.
Pour blue Curaçao into a big martini glass,*
tilt the glass and swirl the liquid until the blue
covers the entire shell.* Pour out excess.
Strain the contents of the cocktail shaker
into the martini glass. Garnish with a lemon
twist. The drink should be a consistent
light blue.

*See glossary.

## Playboy Martini

1 1/2 ounces Starbucks Coffee Liqueur
2 ounces Finlandia vodka
Heavy sweetened cream*
Semisweet or dark chocolate shavings

Garnish: sipping straw

Fill a cocktail shaker with ice. Add
coffee liqueur; stir and strain into
a big martini glass.* Fill the shaker
with clean ice. Add vodka, stir, and
then gently strain using a spoon to
layer* on top of the chilled coffee
liqueur. To top it off, gently pour on
a layer* of heavy sweetened cream.
Finish with a few sprinkles of
chocolate shavings. You should see
3 layers in the martini glass. Serve
with a little straw to allow your guests
to stir it up themselves if they like.

*See glossary.

## Peach Tini

2 ounces Stoli Persik (peach) vodka
1 ounce peach nectar or syrup from canned peaches
1 ounce peach liqueur
1/2 peach

Garnish: wedge of fresh peach

Fill a cocktail shaker with ice. Add vodka, peach nectar
or syrup, and peach liqueur. Add peach half, then muddle.*
Strain into a big martini glass.* Garnish with a wedge of
fresh peach when in season.

*See glossary.

## Sonic Green Martini

3 ounces Finlandia vodka
1 ounce Midori melon liqueur
Splash ($1/4$ ounce) of Rose's lime juice

Garnish: maraschino cherry

Fill a cocktail shaker with ice.
Add vodka, Midori and lime juice.
Stir and strain into a big martini glass.*
Garnish by dropping in a maraschino cherry.

## Copa-Banana Martini

3 ounces Finlandia vodka
1 ounce banana liqueur
1 ounce pineapple juice
Splash ($1/4$ ounce) of fresh
      sweet-and-sour mix*

Garnish: dried banana chips

Fill a cocktail shaker with ice. Add vodka, banana liqueur, pineapple juice and sweet-and-sour mix. Shake and strain into a big martini glass.* Garnish with a healthy pinch of dried banana chips.

*See glossary.                     **37**

## Smokey Bigs Martini

4 ounces Grey Goose vodka
1/2 ounce Lagavulin 16 year Scottish whiskey

Garnish: large caper berry

Fill a cocktail shaker with ice. Add vodka and
scottish whiskey. Stir and strain into a big martini
glass.* Garnish with a large caper berry.

For those who enjoy a good smoke
with their drink.

*See glossary.

## Mandarin-Basil Tini

3 ounces Absolut Mandrin vodka
3/4 ounce fresh sweet-and-sour mix*
1 ounce canned mandarin juice
6 small mandarin orange segments,
          fresh or canned
2 large basil leaves

Garnish: mandarin orange segments,
          basil sprig

Fill a cocktail shaker with ice. Add
vodka, sweet-and-sour mix, mandarin
juice, mandarin orange segments and
basil leaves. Muddle* together, then
strain the contents into a big martini
glass* to create this unique floral
martini. Garnish with mandarins and
a sprig of basil on an olive pick.

*See glossary.

## Mocha Tini

2 1/2 ounces Finlandia vodka
1 ounce Starbucks Coffee Liqueur
1 ounce Godiva chocolate liqueur
Canned whipped cream

Garnish: espresso beans

Fill a cocktail shaker with ice. Add vodka,
coffee liqueur and chocolate liqueur.
Stir and strain into a big martini glass.*
Top liberally with whipped cream.
Garnish with espresso beans.

## Florida Keys Martini

3 ounces Finlandia vodka
1 1/2 ounces freshly squeezed
orange juice
1/2 ounce freshly squeezed
grapefruit juice

Garnish: orange wedge or
orange twist*

Fill a cocktail shaker with ice.
Add vodka, orange juice and
grapefruit juice. Stir and strain
into a big martini glass.*
Garnish with an orange wedge
or orange twist.

Good for retirees and those
needing their daily vitamin C.

*See glossary.

## Pear-a-dox Martini

3 ounces Bombay gin
Splash ($1/4$ ounce) of Hennessy VS cognac
1 $1/2$ ounces pear nectar (or syrup from canned pears)
2 fresh pear wedges, peeled

Garnish: fresh pear wedge

Fill a cocktail shaker with ice. Add gin, cognac and pear nectar.
Add peeled pear wedges and muddle.* Shake and strain into
a big martini glass.* Garnish with a fresh pear wedge on the rim
of the glass (slit the pear in the middle so it will stay anchored).

## Vanilla Martini

3 ounces Stolichnaya Vanil vodka
1 ounce crème de cacao liqueur
$1/2$ ounce Navan vanilla cognac

Garnish: vanilla bean or cinnamon stick

Fill a cocktail shaker with ice. Add vodka,
crème de cacao and cognac. Stir until
your mouth begins to water. Then strain
into a big martini glass* and garnish with
a vanilla bean or cinnamon stick.

*See glossary.

## Feng-Shui Martini

2 ounces Grey Goose vodka
2 ounces Beefeater gin
1 ounce fresh sweet-and-sour mix*
Orange twist*

Fill a cocktail shaker with ice. Add vodka,
gin and sweet-and-sour mix. Stir. Run
the orange twist around the rim of a big
martini glass;* drop the twist into the
glass. Strain the contents of the cocktail
shaker into the glass.

*See glossary.

# $100 Martini

3 ounces Ultimat vodka
1 ounce Hennessy Paradis cognac
1 ounce Grand Marnier Cuvée du Cent Cinquantenaire
                    (150-Year Anniversary)

Fill a cocktail shaker with ice. Add vodka, cognac and
Grand Marnier. Stir and strain into a big martini glass.*


# Las Vegas Martini

4 ounces Finlandia vodka
1 ounce Goldschlager cinnamon-flavored schnapps

Garnish: playing card

Fill a cocktail shaker with ice. Add vodka and schnapps.
Stir and strain into a big martini glass.* Take a small
playing card, cut halfway through the card with scissors,
and attach it to the rim of the glass.

It's hot and quite flashy for those willing to bet.

*See glossary.


# Praline Tini

3 ounces Finlandia vodka
1 ounce praline liqueur
Heavy sweetened cream*

Fill a cocktail shaker with ice.
Add vodka and praline liqueur.
Stir and strain into a big martini
glass.* Finish with a layer* of
heavy sweetened cream.

## Dirty Girl Scout Tini

3 ounces Crater Lake Hazelnut Espresso vodka
1 ounce Godiva chocolate liqueur
Splash ($1/4$ ounce) of white crème de menthe
Lime wedge
Graham cracker crumbs
Heavy sweetened cream*

Fill a cocktail shaker with ice. Pour vodka and chocolate liqueur into the shaker. Add crème de menthe and stir. Rim* a big martini glass* with lime wedge and graham cracker crumbs. Strain the contents of the cocktail shaker into the martini glass. Gently float a layer* of heavy sweetened cream on top.

*See glossary.

## John Wayne

3 ounces Maker's Mark whisky
1 ounce Disaronno Originale amaretto
2 orange wedges

Garnish: orange wheel* or orange twist*

Fill a cocktail shaker with ice.
Add whisky and amaretto. Add
2 orange wedges and muddle.*
Strain into a big martini glass.*
Garnish with an orange wheel
or orange twist.

*See glossary.

## Kingston Martini

2 ounces Finlandia vodka
1 ounce Bacardi Silver rum
1 ounce Midori melon liqueur
1 ounce pineapple juice

Garnish: maraschino cherry

Fill a cocktail shaker with ice. Add vodka, rum, Midori and pineapple juice. Stir and strain into a big martini glass.* Garnish with a maraschino cherry.

*See glossary.

"No woman no cry, Nooooh woman no cry."

## Key Lime Martini

3 ounces Stolichnaya Vanil vodka
1 ounce white crème de cacao liqueur
Splash ($1/4$ ounce) of fresh lime juice
Splash ($1/4$ ounce) of heavy sweetened cream*
Lime wedge
Graham cracker crumbs

Fill a cocktail shaker with ice. Add vodka, crème de cacao, lime juice and heavy sweetened cream. Let stand while rimming* a big martini glass* with lime wedge and graham cracker crumbs. Shake and strain the contents of the cocktail shaker into the martini glass. If you like, garnish with graham cracker crumbs.

Makes giving up dessert easy.

*See glossary.

## Lemon Tini

4 ounces Skyy Citrus vodka
Splash ($^1/4$ ounce) of Grand Marnier
2 lemon wedges

Garnish: lemon twist*

Fill a cocktail shaker with ice. Add vodka,
Grand Marnier and lemon wedges. Muddle,*
stir and then strain into a big martini glass.*
Garnish with a tangy lemon twist.

*See glossary.

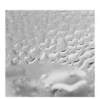

## French 75 Martini

3 ounces Bombay Sapphire gin
Splash ($\frac{1}{4}$ ounce) of fresh sweet-and-sour mix*
1 sugar cube
Bitters
1 ounce champagne

For this classic drink, fill a cocktail shaker with ice.
Add gin and sweet-and-sour mix. Stir and let stand.
Place a sugar cube infused[†] with bitters in the
bottom of a big martini glass.* Strain the contents
of the cocktail shaker into the glass and top off
with champagne. C'est la vie.

[†]To infuse sugar cube, place on a spoon and
add 3 to 4 drops of bitters to the cube.

*See glossary.

## Jill-Tini

3 ounces Finlandia vodka
1 ounce Parfait Amour
1/2 ounce Cointreau orange liqueur
1 ounce fresh sweet-and-sour mix*
1 ounce 7 UP

Garnish: maraschino cherry

Fill a cocktail shaker with ice. Add vodka,
Parfait Amour, Cointreau and sweet-and-sour mix.
Stir vigorously. Pour 7 UP into a big martini glass.*
Strain the contents of the cocktail shaker into
the glass. Garnish with a maraschino cherry.

(Highlighted on the Food Network; named after
Jill Cordes, host of "The Best of…Cocktails.")

## Purple Haze

2 ounces Finlandia vodka
1 ounce Chambord Liqueur
1 ounce Grand Marnier

Garnish: lime wedge

Fill a cocktail shaker with ice. Add vodka,
Chambord and Grand Marnier. Shake
vigorously, then strain into a big martini glass.*
Garnish with a lime wedge.

*See glossary.                                        **63**

## Blessed Martini

2 to 3 drops of blue Curaçao
1 sugar cube
3 ounces absinthe liqueur
3 ounces blessed chilled water
      (preferably blessed by any
      ordained minister)

Pour Curaçao into the bottom of a big martini glass.* Lay a spoon across the top of the glass and place the sugar cube in the spoon. Carefully pour absinthe over the sugar cube, filling the spoon and letting the excess go into the glass, partially dissolving the sugar. Carefully light the sugar cube with a match and let it burn down and dissolve into the martini. After the sugar has caramelized and the flame has gone out, slowly pour blessed chilled water over the sugar that remains in the spoon. Remove the spoon and enjoy.

This drink tastes slightly like black licorice, but beware, it is a version of the concoction that is rumored to have caused Van Gogh to cut off part of his left ear.

*See glossary.

## Blue Nun Martini

2 lemon wedges
1 ounce Grey Goose vodka
3 ounces Hpnotiq liqueur (a blend of vodka,
      cognac and tropical juices)
1 ounce fresh sweet-and-sour mix*

Garnish: orange and lemon twists*

Fill a cocktail shaker with ice. Place lemon wedges in the shaker and muddle* them. Pour in vodka and Hpnotiq. Add sweet-and-sour mix. Shake and strain into a big martini glass.* Garnish with twists of orange and lemon.

## Jell-O Tini

1 3-ounce package Jell-O, green apple or any fruity flavor
3 ounces Finlandia lime vodka, plus more to make gelatin
$\frac{1}{2}$ ounce Grand Marnier

Garnish: lime wheel* or lime twist*

Follow the package directions to make the gelatin, substituting vodka for half of the water. Pour 2 ounces of the warm gelatin into a big martini glass* and refrigerate for 4 to 6 hours, or until it is firm and chilled. Fill a cocktail shaker with ice. Add 3 ounces vodka and the Grand Marnier. Shake and strain into the martini glass. Garnish with a lime wheel or lime twist. We serve this one with an ice cream spoon so you can have your drink and dessert at the same time!

*See glossary.

## Victoria's Martini

3 ounces Absolut Mandrin vodka
2 ounces strong orange spice tea, chilled

Garnish: lemon wedge

Fill a cocktail shaker with ice. Add vodka
laced with tea. Shake and strain into a big
martini glass.* Garnish with a healthy
lemon wedge.

*See glossary.

## Carrot Cake Martini

2 1/2 ounces Kahlúa coffee liqueur
1 ounce Finlandia vodka
1 1/2 ounces Jägermeister liqueur
Lime wedge
Graham cracker crumbs
3/4 ounce Bacardi 151 rum
2 pinches of ground cinnamon
2 pinches of ground nutmeg
Heavy sweetened cream*

Garnish: finely grated carrot

Fill a cocktail shaker with ice. Add Kahlúa,
vodka and Jägermeister to the shaker.
Rim* a big martini glass* with lime wedge
and graham cracker crumbs. Pour rum
directly into the bottom of the martini glass.
Using a match, very carefully light the rum.
Sprinkle cinnamon and nutmeg over the
flames. Shake and strain the contents of
the cocktail shaker into the martini glass.
Gently float a layer* of heavy sweetened
cream on top. Garnish with a small pinch
of grated carrot.

## Hot Havana Tini

2 ounces Bacardi Vanilla rum
2 ounces Captain Morgan spiced rum
1 ounce fresh orange juice
Splash (1/4 ounce) of fresh sweet-and-sour mix*
Lime wedge
Granulated sugar
1/2 ounce Bacardi 151 rum
Pinch of ground cinnamon
Pinch of ground nutmeg

Fill a cocktail shaker with ice. Pour in vanilla
rum and spiced rum. Add orange juice
and sweet-and-sour mix. Rim* a big martini
glass* with lime wedge and granulated sugar
(do not use confectioners' or superfine
(baker's) sugar, as it will not caramelize).
Pour Bacardi 151 into the martini glass. Light
the 151 with a match; gently swirl the contents
around the inside of the glass so that the flame
burns over the sugar (caramelizes) on the rim
of the glass. Do this for approximately
20 seconds, then carefully set the glass down.
Sprinkle cinnamon and nutmeg over the lit
martini glass, then shake and strain the contents
of the cocktail shaker into the still-lit glass.

*See glossary.

## Flir-Tini

3 ounces Bacardi Vanilla rum
2 ounces Baileys Irish Cream
1/2 ounce white crème de cacao liqueur

Fill a cocktail shaker with ice. Add
rum, Irish Cream and crème de cacao.
Shake vigorously and strain into a big
martini glass.* As it says in Tini Bigs'
menu, "Garnish with someone else's
phone number."

## Como Loco Tini

3 ounces Finlandia vodka
1 ounce Grand Marnier
1 ounce fresh sweet-and-sour mix*
Splash ($1/4$ ounce) of fresh orange juice
2 lime wedges

Garnish: lime wedge

Fill a cocktail shaker with ice. Add
vodka, Grand Marnier, sweet-and-sour
mix and orange juice. Add 2 lime wedges
and muddle.* Shake and strain into
a big martini glass.* Garnish with
a wedge of lime.

*See glossary.

## Backyard Martini

4 ounces Skyy Berry vodka
1 ounce fresh cranberry juice

Garnish: 2 lime wedges

Fill a cocktail shaker with ice.
Add vodka and cranberry juice.
Shake vigorously and strain
into a big martini glass.*
Garnish with lime wedges.
It's as easy as running
through the sprinkler.

## Mexi Tini

2 ounces Jose Cuervo Especial tequila
2 ounces cranberry juice
Splash ($1/4$ ounce) of Grand Marnier
1 gummy worm

Fill a cocktail shaker with ice.
Add tequila, cranberry juice and
Grand Marnier. Place gummy worm
in the bottom of a big martini glass.*
Stir and strain the contents of
the cocktail shaker into the glass.
You'll soon begin to hear the
mariachi band in the background.

*See glossary.                    **71**

## Rose Martini

4 ounces Hendrick's gin
Spritz of rose water

Garnish: dried or fresh rose petals

Fill a cocktail shaker with ice. Pour gin into the
shaker and stir vigorously. Place rose water in
an atomizer* and lightly spray the inside of an
empty big martini glass.* Strain the contents
of the cocktail shaker into the martini glass.
Float rose petals on top.

*See glossary.

## Spanish Tini

2 ounces Starbucks Coffee Liqueur
Splash ($1/4$ ounce) of Tia Maria coffee liqueur
2 $1/2$ ounces black coffee, chilled
Lime wedge
Granulated sugar
$1/2$ ounce Bacardi 151 rum
Pinch of ground nutmeg
Pinch of ground cinnamon
Heavy sweetened cream*

Garnish: finely grated semisweet or dark chocolate shavings

Fill a cocktail shaker with ice. Add coffee liqueurs and coffee.
Stir vigorously. Let stand.
Rim* a big martini glass* with lime wedge and granulated sugar
(do not use confectioners' or superfine granulated (baker's) sugar, as
it will not caramelize). Pour rum into the bottom of the martini glass.
Tilt the glass and light the rum with a match. Carefully tilt and swirl
the glass to caramelize the sugar. When the sugar is caramelized, set
the glass down, still ignited, and sprinkle with nutmeg and cinnamon
(you will see small sparks—don't be alarmed). Now strain the contents
of the cocktail shaker into the lit glass. Pour a layer* of heavy
sweetened cream on top. Garnish with chocolate shavings.

*See glossary.

# Democrat Tini

2 ounces Skyy Spiced vodka
1 ounce cranberry juice
2 ounces apple schnapps

Garnish: American flag pick

Fill a cocktail shaker with ice.
Add United Nations-approved
vodka and a union-card-size
pour of cranberry juice,
punch-carded with apple
schnapps. Stir and strain into
a big martini glass.* Garnish
with an American flag pick.

*See glossary.

## Republican Tini

2 ounces Skyy Spiced vodka
1 ounce cranberry juice
2 ounces apple schnapps

Garnish: American flag pick

Fill a cocktail shaker with ice.
Add a conservative pour of vodka,
a government-size contract of cranberry
juice, and classified apple schnapps.
Stir and strain into a big martini glass.*
Garnish with an American flag pick.

*See glossary.

# Jolly Tini

4 ounces Finlandia vodka infused with
apple-flavored Jolly Ranchers[†]
3/4 ounce fresh sweet-and-sour mix[*]

Fill a cocktail shaker with ice. Add infused
vodka and sweet-and-sour mix. Stir vigorously
and strain into a big martini glass.[*]

Option: Garnish with 1 maraschino cherry.

[†]To infuse vodka, place 18 Jolly Ranchers in
a 750-ml bottle of vodka. Let stand until the
candies dissolve, about 24 hours, rotating the
bottle 2 to 3 times.

[*]See glossary.

## Banshee Tini

2 ounces Finlandia vodka
1 ounce Kahlúa coffee liqueur
½ ounce Rumple Minze peppermint schnapps
1 ounce Godiva chocolate liqueur
½ ounce 160-proof Stroh rum

Fill a cocktail shaker with ice. Add vodka, Kahlúa, schnapps, chocolate
liqueur and rum. Yeow! Stir and strain into a big martini glass.*
Only Tini Bigs had the b*lls to come up with this one!

Option: Rim glass with crushed peppermint Altoids.

*See glossary.

Scream like hell after one of these.

## Tini Bigs Lemon Drop

2 $1/2$ ounces Stoli Strasberi vodka
1 $1/2$ ounces Tuaca liqueur
1 ounce fresh sweet-and-sour mix*
3 lemon wedges
Superfine granulated (baker's) sugar

Garnish: lemon wedge

Fill a cocktail shaker with ice. Add vodka, Tuaca and sweet-and-sour mix. Add 2 lemon wedges and muddle.* Rim* a big martini glass* with a lemon wedge and superfine sugar. Shake and strain the contents of the cocktail shaker into the glass. Garnish with a lemon wedge.

*See glossary.

You will notice the "Tini" difference — dee-licious!

## Insomnia-Tini

2 ounces Finlandia vodka
2 ounces energy drink with guarana
Splash ($1/4$ ounce) of fresh grapefruit juice
Splash ($1/4$ ounce) of fresh orange juice

Fill a cocktail shaker with ice. Add vodka
and jump-start with a healthy pour of energy
drink, grapefruit juice and orange juice.
Stir and strain into a big martini glass.*
Not to be taken if going to bed soon!

*See glossary.

## Ménage à Trois Martini

2 ounces Bacardi O rum
1 ounce Disaronno Originale amaretto
1/2 ounce orange juice
1/2 ounce pineapple juice
1/2 ounce fresh sweet-and-sour mix*
1 wedge each of lemon, lime and orange
1 ounce champagne

Fill a cocktail shaker with ice. Pour in rum
and amaretto. Add orange juice, pineapple juice
and sweet-and-sour mix. Add lemon, lime and
orange wedges. Muddle* contents vigorously,
then strain into a big martini glass* and finish
with a gentle pour of champagne on top. Serve
with a twist* — like a true ménage à trois.

*See glossary.

## Sex in the City

3 ounces Finlandia vodka
$^1/_2$ ounce Grand Marnier
2 ounces deep red cranberry juice

Garnish: lime wedge or cranberries

Fill a cocktail shaker with ice.
Add vodka, Grand Marnier and
cranberry juice. Stir vigorously
and strain into a big martini glass.*
Garnish with lime or cranberries.

*See glossary.

## Hangover Martini

2 ounces Absolut Peppar vodka
3 ounces good-quality Bloody Mary mix
Lime wedge
Kosher salt

Garnish: 3 jalapeño-stuffed olives

Fill a cocktail shaker with ice. Add vodka
and Bloody Mary mix. Stir. Rim* a big martini
glass* with lime wedge and kosher salt. Strain
the contents of the cocktail shaker into the
glass. Garnish with olives.

*See glossary.

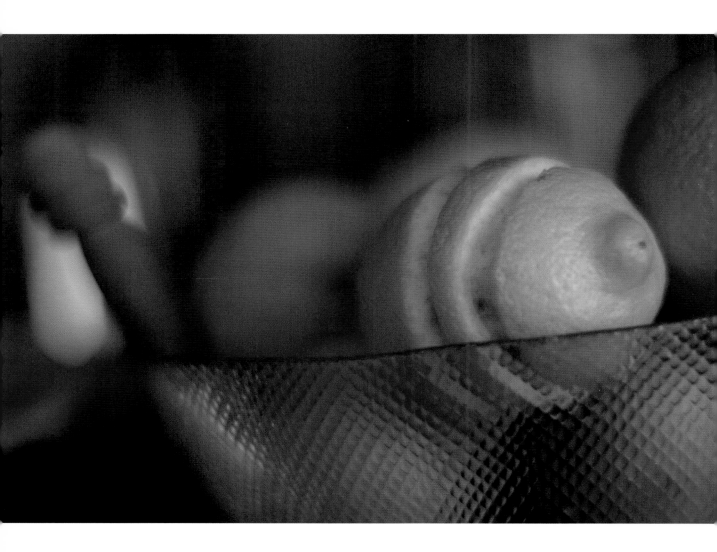

# GLOSSARY

**Atomizer**
This is a small spray bottle filled with a liquid (vermouth, rose water) and pumped to emit a mist that evenly coats the martini glass.

**Big Martini Glass**
Tini Bigs uses a 10-ounce martini glass, or "shell." The recipes in this book are designed for one large martini glass but can easily be split between two smaller martini glasses if you prefer.

**Heavy Sweetened Cream**
In a jar or container with a tight lid, combine 1 part Kahlúa, 1 part rock candy syrup, and 2 parts heavy whipping cream, leaving room for the contents to mix. Shake vigorously until the mixture becomes frothy. Rock candy syrup can be found in most grocery stores where bar mixes are sold.

**Layer**
To float a liquid on the surface of a cocktail, pour it gently over the back of a spoon held close to the drink's surface, letting it spill over to create a separate layer on top of the drink. Layering is usually done with heavy sweetened cream, but can be done with other liquids as well. Each layer of liquid must be thicker than the layer beneath it, or it will seep into the liquor below.

**Muddle**
A small wooden bat called a muddler, approximately 8 to 10 inches in length, is used (the blunt end, not the rounded end) to "mash" the fruit so it releases its pulp and juices into the ice-filled cocktail shaker.

**Rim**
Take a lime wedge and slide it around the rim of a martini glass to coat it in a layer of lime juice. Then turn the glass upside down and place the rim flat on a plate containing sugar or graham cracker crumbs.

**Shell**
The term "shell" refers to the martini glass. See Big Martini Glass.

**Stir**
Use a metal parfait spoon that is long enough to reach the bottom of the cocktail shaker.

**Strainer**
This is a flat, circular tool with a flat handle and a spring that fits snugly on the top of the cocktail shaker, allowing only the spirits and pulp, not the ice, to be released into the martini glass.

**Sweet-and-Sour Mix**
1 cup sugar
1 cup water
1 cup fresh lemon juice
1 cup fresh lime juice
1/4 cup fresh orange juice

Combine sugar and water until all the sugar is dissolved. Add lemon, lime and orange juices and refrigerate.

**Twist**
Make a twist with a zester, a small tool that is used to slice thin strips of peel from citrus fruit without the bitter underlying white pith. Press the prong of the zester against the fruit to create a sliver of peel approximately 3 to 5 inches long.

**Wheel**
Cut horizontally across a citrus fruit to make a circular slice.

## ACKNOWLEDGMENTS

Thanks to the present and past staff at Tini Bigs, for being the foundation of over 3250 consecutive days of business. They make it look easy. Our talented, personable, educated employees, many of whom have become longtime friends, have all contributed to Tini Bigs. Proudly presenting our cocktails to customers who have a little or a lot of martini experience, they are the familiar faces that our patrons come to know and appreciate. Patrick Haight, for your support and creativity and making my life so great. Kathleen Collins, Bill Mcintyre and Matt Dickinson, for caring so much. Alex Rosenast, for being there to bounce ideas and problems back and forth. Josh, Aaron, Kevin, Heather, Tennille, Carla and Marin, for helping create our new recipes and putting in those late nights of research. Mike Gastineau, Dave Grosby and Tom Lykus, for liking martinis and being able to talk to everyone about it. Dennis, for seven years of loyalty to Tini Bigs and providing education to all guests who wanted to be informed. Frank Sinatra and Dean Martin, for making music that makes you want to drink cocktails in glasses that are designed to break. Burt and Norita, for loving me and promoting me and my endeavors always. Peggy, for tolerating all those late nights and that cigar smell. Sean Connery, I'm with you. Tamara, Lori and Lissa, for putting us and keeping us on the map. The Food Network, for being there when I'm hungry. G. M. Ford, for writing the introduction and drinking martinis. Kristen Adams and Brown Forman, for your longtime support and friendship. Allied Domecq, Skyy, Bacardi, Future Brands and Moët Hennessy USA, for providing great products. Dave, Darrell, Frank, C.J., Terry, Rita, Eric, Larry, Bob, Mary, and all our other loyal customers, for your continued quality control. Thank you to the entire Seattle restaurant and bar community for your support.